D1525807

# Lance Armstrong

by Elena Martin

STECK-VAUGHN
Harcourt Supplemental Publishers

www.steck-vaughn.com

# Contents

A Boy and His Bike . . . . 3

The Champ . . . . . . . . . 8

A New Goal . . . . . . . . . 12

Back on the Bike . . . . . . 16

Reaching Out . . . . . . . 20

Timeline . . . . . . . . . . . 24

# A Boy and His Bike

In the 1980s, a boy named Lance Armstrong was growing up in Plano, Texas. He loved any sport where he could move fast. He especially loved riding his bike.

When Lance was in fifth grade, he decided to try running in races. He won his first race.

In sixth grade, Lance tried swimming. At first he was not very good. But Lance kept trying. Soon he was winning swim races, too.

One day, Lance read about a race called IronKids. In this race, kids had to run, swim, and bike. Lance entered the race and won. Then he won many others like it. Lance liked to run and swim, but riding the bike was Lance's favorite part of the race.

Lance and friends get ready for a swim race.

Lance warms up for a race in Japan.

While Lance was still in high school, he was asked to join a special team. The team was going to Russia to race against the best bike riders in the world. Lance's love of bike riding was taking him far away from Plano, Texas!

Lance and his coach celebrate his win in Italy.

Lance did not win the race in Russia. But one year later, Lance came in eleventh in an important race in Japan. One year after that, he won first place in a road race in Italy. Lance was on his way to becoming a champion!

# The Champ

Lance leads the pack at a race in 1991.

By 1991, Lance was winning many bike races. Lance liked being a winner. He practiced even harder. Lance dreamed of winning a medal in the Olympics someday.

In 1992, Lance took a step toward his dream. He raced in the Olympics, but he did not win. Later that year, he rode in another big race.

Instead of racing on a track like he had in the Olympics, he rode on rough roads. Lance and the other racers had to pedal up big hills and ride in the rain. Lance was not used to such a tough race. He came in last!

Lance uses his energy to take the lead.

Lance trained harder. He practiced riding on big hills and bumpy roads. He even rode on cold, rainy days.

Lance's coach showed him how to plan out each race. Lance learned when to follow other bike riders to save his energy. He also learned when to pedal fast and hard to take the lead.

Lance celebrates after winning the day's race.

Soon people were saying that Lance was the best bike rider in the world. He won many races and more than a million dollars in prize money. He was the youngest road-racing champion ever!

# A New Goal

Years of training make Lance stronger and faster.

For the next few years, Lance spent most of his time training and racing in Europe. He trained hard by riding all day long. Each year Lance rode better and better.

Lance races for the U.S. Olympic team in 1996.

In 1996, Lance returned to the United States. This time, the Olympics were being held in Georgia. Everyone thought that Lance would win.

But Lance was feeling sick. He was used to riding with aches and pains, so he did his best. Lance finished the race, but he did not do well.

Lance's doctor gave him special medicine to cure his cancer.

Over the next few months, the pain got worse.
Finally, Lance went to the doctor. The doctor said
that Lance had a disease called cancer. Lance
needed an operation. He would have to take
special medicine to kill the cancer in his body.

His friends and his coach helped Lance fight against cancer.

Lance knew that the medicine would make him weak and cause his hair to fall out. Lance also knew that he would die if the medicine did not work.

Lance never gave up when he was racing. He would not give up now. Lance had a new goal. He had to fight to get well. His doctors, nurses, friends, and family were there to help him fight and win!

# Back on the Bike

For months, Lance took his medicine. He got so weak that he slept for 20 hours some days. But Lance did not give up.

Slowly, Lance got better. Then tests showed that the cancer was gone! Lance got back on his bike as soon as he could.

Lance's friends often rode with him. They rode very, very slowly. They did not want Lance to know that they could now ride faster and farther than he could.

But every day, Lance got back on his bike. His legs got stronger. He pedaled faster and faster. He wanted to show the world that he had beaten cancer. He made a plan to race again!

Lance rides again after winning his fight against cancer.

Lance races in the Tour de France in 1999.

In 1998, Lance joined a bike team. The team went to Europe to train. Once again, Lance was riding on big hills and bumpy roads! He came in fourteenth in his first big race. People were surprised that he did so well.

Lance kept training hard, and he began winning. In 1999, he entered the toughest bike race of all. This race was the Tour de France.

Lance wins the 1999 Tour de France.

The race was more than 2,000 miles long. The riders pedaled through mountains, on country roads, and through city streets. The whole race took about 20 days.

Lance won the Tour de France that year. He also won it again for the next three years! Today Lance is one of the most famous sports stars in the world.

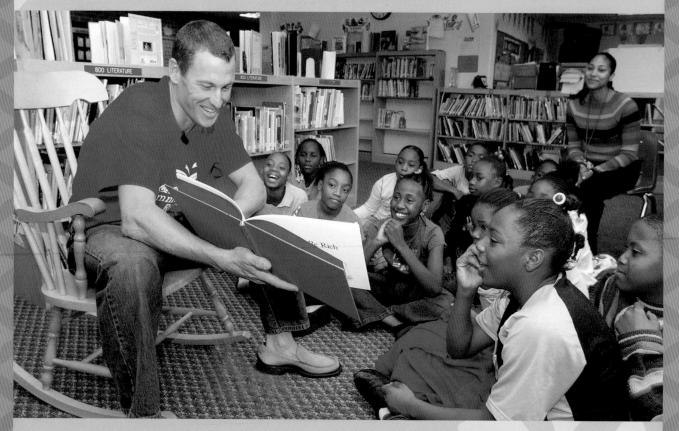

Lance reads to a group of children.

Before Lance got sick, he thought mostly about winning races. But having cancer changed Lance. He saw that other things were important, too.

Lance decided to help other people. He wanted to help those who had cancer. Since Lance was well known, he thought that people would listen to him.

Lance meets many people at the Ride for the Roses race each year.

Lance began raising money. He set up a special bike race called Ride for the Roses. This race is held each year.

In 2002, this event raised more than $2,000,000! The money is given to people who have cancer as well as doctors who study the disease.

LE TOUR DE FRANCE

Lance celebrates a win with his son, Luke.

Lance also changed the way he lived. He had learned how important friends and family are. He got married. He became a father. Today one of his favorite things to do is to make pancakes for his children.

Lance still has many dreams for the future.

Lance says that he is a better man now than he was before he had cancer. He is looking forward to watching his children grow up. He wants to win more races, and he wants to see more and more people with cancer get well.

# Timeline

**1971**
Lance is born on
September 18.

**1984**
Lance wins his first
triathlon at age 13.

**1989**
Lance joins the
Junior National
Cycling Team.

**1992**
Lance races in the
Olympics and places 14th.

**1996**
Lance learns
he has cancer.

**1998**
Lance joins the U.S. Postal
Service Pro Cycling Team.

**1999**
Lance wins the Tour de France
for the first time.

**2000**
Lance wins the
Tour de France again.

**2001**
Lance wins his third
Tour de France.

**2002**
Lance wins the Tour de France
for the fourth time.